D0577943

Getting To Know...

Nature's Children

WALRUS

Laima Dingwall

PUBLISHER	Joseph R. DeVarennes
PUBLICATION DIRECTOR	Kenneth H. Pearson
MANAGING EDITOR	Valerie Wyatt
SERIES ADVISOR	Merebeth Switzer
SERIES CONSULTANT	Michael Singleton
CONSULTANTS	Ross James
	Kay McKeever
	Dr. Audrey N. Tomera
ADVISORS	Roger Aubin
	Robert Furlonger
	Gaston Lavoie
EDITORIAL SUPERVISOR	Jocelyn Smyth
PRODUCTION MANAGER	Ernest Homewood
PRODUCTION ASSISTANTS	Penelope Moir
	Brock Piper

EDITORS

Katherine Farris   Anne Minguet-Patocka
Sandra Gulland   Sarah Reid
Cristel Kleitsch   Cathy Ripley
Elizabeth MacLeod   Eleanor Tourtel
Pamela Martin   Karin Velcheff

PHOTO EDITORS	Bill Ivy
	Don Markle
DESIGN	Annette Tatchell
CARTOGRAPHER	Jane Davie
PUBLICATION ADMINISTRATION	Kathy Kishimoto
	Monique Lemonnier

ARTISTS

Marianne Collins   Greg Ruhl
Pat Ivy   Mary Theberge

This series is approved and recommended by the Federation of Ontario Naturalists.

Canadian Cataloguing in Publication Data

Dingwall, Laima, 1953-
  Walrus

(Getting to know—nature's children)
Includes index.
ISBN 0-7172-1938-0

1. Walruses—Juvenile literature.
I. Title. II. Series.

QL737.P62D56 1985   j599.74'7   C85-098741-5

Copyright © 1985 by Grolier Limited. All rights reserved.
Printed and Bound in U.S.A.

Have you ever wondered . . .

Most people cannot help but smile when they see a walrus. Maybe the walrus's comical face, complete with a bristly mustache, is what does it. Or perhaps it is the friendly way the walrus has of snuggling up to its neighbors on the ice.

But there is more to the walrus than first meets the eye. If you could visit the Arctic coast where the walrus lives, you would see that this big funny looking animal is actually a superb cold-weather survivor. Let's take a closer look at how the walrus lives.

The coarse whiskers on its muzzle are the only hair an adult walrus has.

Meet the Family

If the walrus held a family reunion for its North American relatives, who would come? Its cousins the sea lion and the seal, of course.

The walrus and its cousins belong to a group of animals called the pinnipeds. The word *pinniped* means "flipper feet." Because pinnipeds spend much of their time in the ocean, flippers are much more useful to them than ordinary legs.

Although walruses and their relatives are sea-living animals, they are not at all like fish. Fish breathe through gills and spend all their lives underwater. Walruses have lungs, just as you do, and must come to the surface to breathe air. As well, fish are cold-blooded and walruses are warm-blooded. That means that fish take on the temperature of the water around them. Walruses, like you, have a body temperature that stays more or less the same.

Up for air.

What Big Teeth You Have!

It is easy to tell walruses from their relatives. They are the only ones with tusks.

Their tusks are really two very long teeth, one at each corner of the mouth. They start growing soon after the walrus is born. By the time the walrus is two years old, its tusks are 10 centimetres (4 inches) long. An adult male walrus might have tusks as long as one metre (3 feet), each weighing almost as much as a good-sized watermelon. Of course, you cannot see all of a walrus's tusks. Part of them are hidden inside its mouth.

Male tusks

Female tusks

The size of a bull's tusks is important. In any argument with other males, the bull with the longest tusks usually gets his way.

All-Purpose Tusks

In addition to its tusks the walrus has 16 other teeth. All of these teeth are quite small. Why are its tusks so large? Because they are useful. The walrus uses them to rake through the sea bottom when it is looking for food. And, because tusks are strong and almost impossible to break, they make fierce weapons. The walrus uses them to defend itself against predators such as the Polar Bear or Killer Whale.

Tusks also make handy grappling hooks when the walrus wants to climb out of the water onto a slippery ice floe. The walrus simply stabs its tusks into the ice and hoists itself over the edge. And for getting around on land, tusks are particularly helpful. The walrus uses its tusks like ski poles, sticking them into the ice and pulling itself along.

A walrus uses its tusks the way a mountain climber uses a pick.

Walruses East and West

Two kinds of walruses live in North America:
the Pacific Walrus and the Atlantic Walrus.

The Pacific Walrus lives on the western edge
of the Arctic Ocean, near Alaska. The Atlantic
Walrus makes its home on the eastern edge of
the Arctic Ocean, near Hudson Bay and
Labrador.

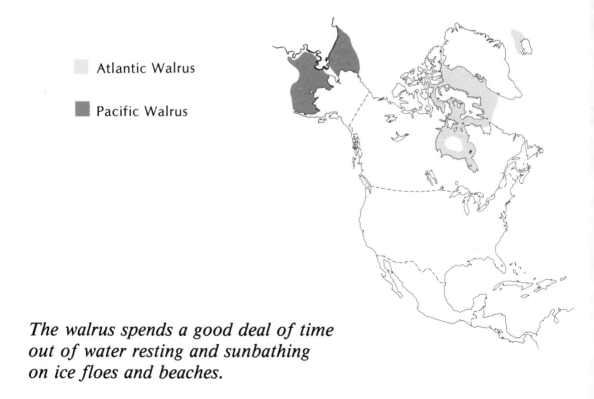

Atlantic Walrus

Pacific Walrus

The walrus spends a good deal of time
out of water resting and sunbathing
on ice floes and beaches.

As Big As A . . . Walrus!

The French explorer Jacques Cartier saw walruses on his early voyages to North America. When he wrote about them later, he called them "great beasts . . . like large oxen."

No wonder. The walrus is HUGE. A full-grown male Pacific Walrus weighs 1100 kilograms (2400 pounds) or more. And from the tips of its whiskers to the end of its tail, it might be as long as four metres (13 feet). In other words, the walrus weighs about as much as 14 full-grown adult men and is as long as a large car.

The Atlantic Walrus is slightly smaller. It weighs on average 900 kilograms (2000 pounds) and measures about three metres (10 feet) long.

Hauling out.

Walruses Love Water

Everything about the walrus is suited to life in water. Does the shape of the walrus's body remind you of an oversized fish? That streamlined shape helps the walrus cut through the water easily and quickly.

You could be excused for not noticing the walrus's ears. They are small, tiny slits on the sides of its head. When the walrus dives underwater, a flap of skin automatically closes over each ear to keep out water. And the walrus does not need to worry about getting water up its nose either. A fold of skin covers its nostrils when it dives, just like built-in nose plugs.

Cold-Water Comfort

You might find swimming in cold Arctic water a chilling experience. Not the walrus. Its tough leathery skin covers a thick layer—up to 15 centimetres (6 inches) thick—of special fat called blubber. Blubber is like a warm parka for the walrus; it keeps the walrus warm not only in icy water but also in chilly air.

The walrus's large, flat head is particularly useful when it is swimming under the ice. If the walrus needs to come to the surface for a breath of air, it uses its head as a battering ram to make a hole in the ice.

A walrus rests at sea in a vertical position. Two inflatable air sacs in its neck keep its bulky head above water.

Walrus Underwater

The walrus has two pairs of flippers—one near the front of its body and another pair in the back. Its front flippers have five long "fingers" joined by webs of skin. When the walrus spreads these fingers, the flippers become wide, powerful paddles for lots of swimming power.

The walrus uses its rear flippers like the rudder on a boat. They help it to change directions when it is in the water.

Walrus flipper

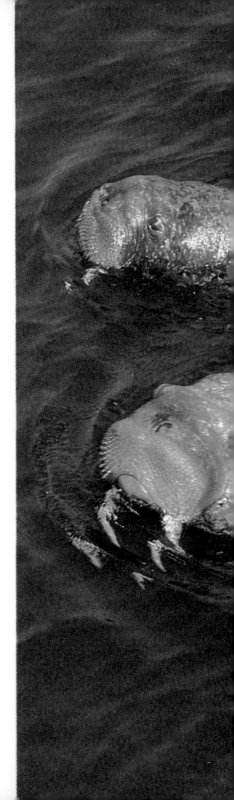

A walrus's layer of blubber not only keeps it warm, it helps it to float.

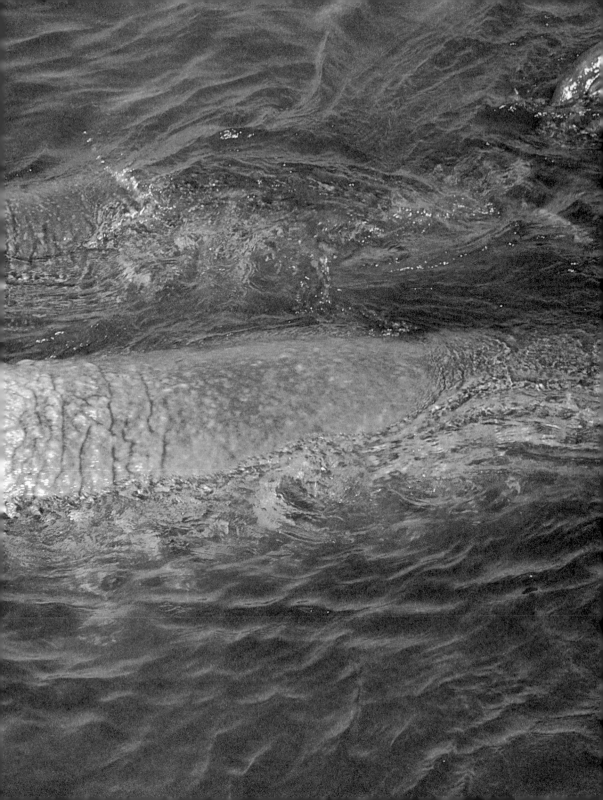

Dive, Dive, Dive

The walrus dives underwater to find food and to escape predators. It usually finds its food in shallow water close to shore, but it can dive as deep as 90 metres (300 feet). It can also stay underwater for as long as 15 minutes without coming up for air. Whew!

How does the walrus do it? After all, walruses don't breath through gills as fish do. They have lungs: they need air.

When a walrus is underwater its muscles relax and its heart rate slows down. That way it uses up the supply of air in its lungs slowly. This allows it to stay underwater for a long time.

The walrus is a very graceful swimmer—and a fast one. It can reach speeds up to 24 kilometres (15 miles) per hour in the water. That is about five times the speed of the fastest human swimmer.

Because walruses are bottom feeders, they prefer shallow waters less than 18 metres (60 feet) deep.

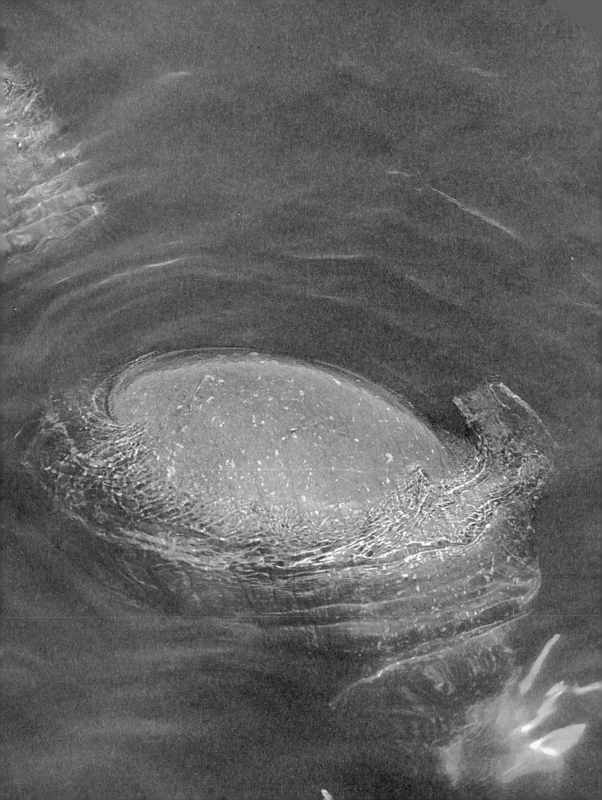

Thump, Thump, Thump

The walrus may be graceful in the water, but on land it is a different story. There, it humps along like an overgrown caterpillar.

The walrus uses its short, but very sturdy flippers to push itself along the ground. It can swing its back flippers forward and fan them out to brace itself. This way, it can push itself up and forward with a lunging thump.

If the walrus is in a hurry, it hooks its tusks into the ice and pulls itself forward. The walrus may look clumsy and comical as it waddles and thumps along, but it can reach surprising speeds when it is pursuing an intruder or escaping danger.

Walruses will sometimes wait for the tide to lift them up onto a rocky ledge.

Ask a Walrus to Dinner

A walrus will eat almost any small creatures it can find on the sea bottom. It often eats shrimps, whelks, marine worms and sea cucumbers. But its favorite food, and the mainstay of its diet, is clams.

How does a walrus find clams in the sand on the ocean bottom? It rakes up the bottom with its tusks and searches through it with its bristly mustache.

That mustache is made up of some 400 very stiff, thick, strong hairs arranged in neat rows. Each hair is about as long as a broomstraw and tipped with sensitive nerves. That is like having 400 extra fingers to help you find food.

The walrus is a very delicate eater. It can eat clams without swallowing any of the shell. No one has ever figured out how it can do this.

Scientists used to think that the walrus cracked the clam shells with its back teeth, then spat them out and swallowed the meat. But now they think that somehow the walrus sucks the soft clam meat right out of the shell, using its tongue and thick, rubbery lips.

Opposite page:

These long tusks are just great for clam-digging.

Wall-to-Wall Walrus

After a good feed, a walrus usually likes to haul itself out of the water to rest or snooze in the sun. A group of walruses often has its own favorite *oogli*. That is what Inuit call the place where walruses gather. An oogli can be a rocky beach or nothing more than a large ice floe surrounded by deep water.

No matter what or where the oogli is, one thing is sure. The oogli is always crowded with walruses. In fact, sometimes so many walruses snuggle so closely together that it is hard to tell where one walrus stops and another starts. They look like one big walrus carpet.

Warring Walruses

With so many walruses gathered together on the same oogli, it is not surprising that arguments sometimes break out. At times, walruses squabble so loudly that their bellows can be heard two kilometres (1.5 miles) away.

What do walruses argue about? Perhaps one walrus has rolled over and accidently jabbed another one with its tusks. Or a walrus might fancy sleeping in another walrus's cozy spot.

Sometimes real fights break out. Two walruses will face one another, rear up on their flippers and throw their heads back to threaten each other with their tusks. But such fights rarely come to blows. The walrus with the shorter tusks usually gives way. Soon all the walruses relax and lie quietly together again—until the next squabble.

"Make room for me!"

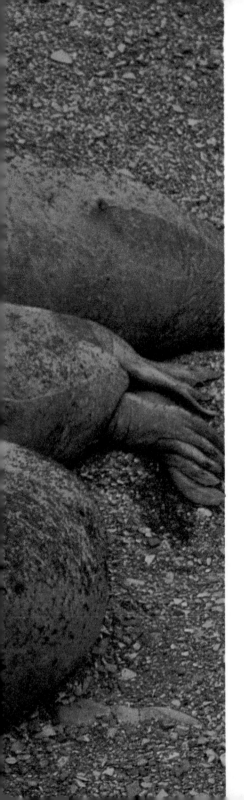

In the Pink

When a walrus hauls itself out of the water onto an oogli, its thick, leathery skin is quite pale and gray. But after it has stretched out in the sun for a few minutes, its skins slowly turns a rosy shade of pink.

No, the walrus is not sunburned. Blood vessels just under its skin expand in the warm sun. Blood rushes into them, and that is what gives the walrus's skin its rosy color.

The More the Merrier

A lone walrus is a sad walrus. Walruses are very social animals and love nothing more than the company of their own kind.

Walruses live and travel in groups. There might be a hundred or more walruses in a group, all mixed together, old and young, male and female. The female walruses are called cows. Males are bulls and the young are—what else?—calves. During breeding season the older bulls drive away the younger ones. These sometimes form their own groups and stay on the edge of the main group.

Walruses sometimes form herds of up to 2000 bulls, cows and calves.

Walrus On The Move

The walrus spends the summer months in the waters along the edge of the Arctic ice. The Pacific Walrus summers along the northern coasts of Siberia and Alaska. Its Atlantic cousin summers on the edge of the Atlantic Arctic.

Come winter, when the northern-most seas start to freeze over, both the Pacific and Atlantic walruses travel south. They migrate to places where the warmer currents and shallower waters keep the ice from closing up the bays and the sea. Sometimes they might do a little ice-hitchhiking. If the big ice floes are heading in the right direction, the walruses will drift along with them.

Once spring rolls around, the walrus travels north again.

When migrating, walruses like to hitch a ride on ice. But if the ice floe heads off in the wrong direction, it is time to start swimming.

Mating Time

After their springtime migration to the far north, it is time for the walruses to mate. First, each male walrus stakes out a territory on an ice floe. A male walrus mates with as many as 30 female walruses in a season. A female walrus, however, usually mates with only one male. All of the females the male has mated with crowd onto his territory. He guards these females and fights off any other bulls that try to come near.

Once mating season is over, the bulls no longer worry about their territories or the other males. In fact, they do not even worry about the females they have so fiercely protected. The females have to raise their young with no help from the fathers.

Walrus Birthday Time

About a year after mating, a female walrus is ready to give birth. If possible, she uses an ice floe near the oogli as her nursery. Usually only one baby is born. Twins are very rare. At birth, a baby walrus is tiny—at least by walrus standards. The newborn walrus weighs from 45 to 70 kilograms (100 to 150 pounds). That is about as heavy as most full-grown women.

The newborn walrus is weak and helpless. Its layer of blubber is very thin, and it has only a coat of short, silvery gray baby hair to protect it from the cold. It is not surprising then that the walrus babies spend much of their time trying to keep warm by cuddling close to their mothers.

As it snuggles next to her, the young walrus nurses often on the mother's thick, creamy milk. It will drink this rich milk until it is almost two years old.

Opposite page:

Calves must stay with their mother until they are two years old. By then they will have developed tusks large enough for feeding.

Walrus Motherhood

The female walrus is an excellent mother. In fact, she will sometimes adopt an orphaned baby walrus and raise it as her own.

The mother walrus and her baby are very affectionate. They spend much of their time giving each other tiny "kisses" by rubbing their bristly mustaches against one another. They even give each other walrus hugs and the mother may hold her baby with her flippers.

A mother walrus tries never to let her baby wander out of her sight. If a baby should get separated from its mother, it cries so loudly that she will soon come to the rescue.

The young walrus can swim soon after it is born. Often it swims side by side with its mother. But sometimes a young calf has a hard time keeping up with its mother. When that happens, the baby will climb onto her back and hold her sides tightly with its flippers. Sometimes it will hitchhike a ride in this way for hours.

Opposite page:

Hitching a ride on mom's back.

Time to Leave Mother

The young walrus is usually safe as long as its mother is nearby. She protects it and teaches it how to find its own food and how to avoid Polar Bears and Killer Whales and other enemies of young walruses. After two years, it is time for the mother to give birth to a new baby and for the young walrus to make a life of its own.

The young walrus sunning itself on the oogli has probably got a long happy life ahead of it. It can go clam-digging, enjoy cold-water swims and snuggle with other walruses for many years to come. Some walruses live to the ripe old age of 30.

Special Words

Blood vessels Tubes, arteries and veins through which blood flows in the body.

Blubber A layer of fat on an animal's body that keeps the cold out and body heat in.

Bull Male walrus.

Calf Baby walrus.

Cow Female walrus.

Flippers Wide flat limbs adapted specially for swimming.

Lungs Parts of the body that take in air and put it into the blood.

Mate To come together to produce young.

Migration A seasonal journey to find food or a place to mate and bear young.

Oogli Inuit word for a walrus gathering place.

Territory Area that an animal or group of animals lives in and often defends from other animals of the same kind.

Tusks Two elongated pointed teeth that extend outside the walrus's mouth.

INDEX

Cover Photo: Stephen J. Krasemann (Valan Photos)
Photo Credits: Leonard Lee Rue III (Miller Services), page 4; Brian Milne (First Light Associated Photographers), pages 7, 11, 14, 19, 21, 23, 24, 31, 39; Stephen J. Krasemann (Valan Photos), pages 8, 12, 17, 27, 28, 36; Fred Bruemmer, pages 32, 40, 43, 44-45.

Getting To Know...

Nature's Children

HAWKS

Merebeth Switzer

PUBLISHER	Joseph R. DeVarennes
PUBLICATION DIRECTOR	Kenneth H. Pearson
MANAGING EDITOR	Valerie Wyatt
SERIES ADVISOR	Merebeth Switzer
SERIES CONSULTANT	Michael Singleton
CONSULTANTS	Ross James
	Kay McKeever
	Dr. Audrey N. Tomera
ADVISORS	Roger Aubin
	Robert Furlonger
	Gaston Lavoie
EDITORIAL SUPERVISOR	Jocelyn Smyth
PRODUCTION MANAGER	Ernest Homewood
PRODUCTION ASSISTANTS	Penelope Moir
	Brock Piper
EDITORS	Katherine Farris	Anne Minguet-Patocka
	Sandra Gulland	Sarah Reid
	Cristel Kleitsch	Cathy Ripley
	Elizabeth MacLeod	Eleanor Tourtel
	Pamela Martin	Karin Velcheff
PHOTO EDITORS	Bill Ivy
	Don Markle
DESIGN	Annette Tatchell
CARTOGRAPHER	Jane Davie
PUBLICATION ADMINISTRATION	Kathy Kishimoto
	Monique Lemonnier
ARTISTS	Marianne Collins	Greg Ruhl
	Pat Ivy	Mary Theberge

This series is approved and recommended by the Federation of Ontario Naturalists.

Canadian Cataloguing in Publication Data

Switzer, Merebeth.
  Hawks

(Getting to know—nature's children)
Includes index.
ISBN 0-7172-1937-2

1. Hawks—Juvenile literature.
I. Title. II. Series.

QL696.F32S97 1985   j598'.916   C85-098716-4

Copyright © 1985 by Grolier Limited. All rights reserved.
Printed and Bound in U.S.A.

Have you ever wondered . . .

Has anyone ever said to you, "You have eyes like a hawk?" If they have, they mean that you have very sharp eyesight. But no matter how good your eyesight is, it cannot match a hawk's. As they fly overhead, these amazing birds can see the slightest movement in the grass beneath them. Their eyesight is eight to ten times more powerful than ours is.

Good eyesight is important for a hawk. It lives by hunting, and it hunts as it flies or from its perch high up in a tree. So it must be able to spot a likely meal from quite a distance away. But excellent eyesight is just one of the many interesting things about the hawk. Let's find out more about these incredibly sharp-eyed birds.

Swainson's Hawk.

The First Flight

The young hawk stands at the edge of its nest high in a tree and looks down. It is a long way to the ground. In the nest, its brothers and sisters are flapping their wings as if to say, "My turn next."

Then, suddenly, as the young hawk is just about to launch itself out of the nest, it is pushed from behind by an over-eager sister. Down it goes, fluttering and flapping. It lands safely with a gentle thump. Its eyes gleam brightly. It has flown! Now it is ready to take its place in the wonderful world of hawks.

A Red-tailed Hawk chick about to take the leap.

Hawks Everywhere

There is a type of hawk for every habitat in North America. In fact, hawks are found almost everywhere in the world except in Antarctica. They live almost anywhere they can find food. Some types of hawks prefer forests, others grasslands and still others semi-desert areas.

Some hawks have two homes—a summer home where they nest and a winter home. Why? These hawks nest in regions where the winters are cold and many animals hibernate. To find enough food in winter, they must fly south to warmer climates.

The Northern Goshawk lives in the far north and is rarely seen.

The Hawk Family

If you had to draw a family tree of North American hawks it would have five main branches. Each branch would stand for one of the five kinds of hawks—accipiters, buteos, falcons, harriers and ospreys. Some of these main branches would sprout into smaller branches. The buteo branch would have more smaller branches than any other because there are 13 kinds of buteos in North America. The osprey and harrier branches, on the other hand, would have no smaller ones.

You can recognize the different kinds of hawks by the size and shape of their wings and tail.

With their narrow, pointed wings and tapered tail, falcons are built for speed.

The more rounded and shorter wings of the accipiters are ideal for maneuvering through densely forested areas.

The buteos are great soarers thanks to their broad wings and fan-like tail.

The long rounded wings and lengthy tail of the harrier make it a very agile hunter.

The long narrow wings of the osprey appear bowed, much like a gull's.

The osprey is sometimes called "fish hawk" because of its skill at catching fish.

Mini Hawks and Maxi Hawks

You probably think of hawks as quite large birds and indeed some of them are. The osprey, for instance, can reach a length of 65 centimetres (25 inches) and has a wingspan of more than 165 centimetres (65 inches). The Kestrel, on the other hand, is smaller than a robin. This mini falcon is little more than 20 centimetres (8 inches) long.

Generally speaking, hawks are not very colorful birds. They come mainly in shades of bluish gray or brown. Their backs are usually quite dark. Their underparts are lighter to almost white, often marked with bars and speckles. A few hawks, however, have some brighter-colored feathers here or there, and some—such as the Red-tailed Hawk—are even named for these splashes of color.

Unlike many birds, male and female hawks do not look very different. The color of their feathers and their markings are usually the same. But you might know which was which if you saw them together, because the female is slightly larger.

Opposite page:

Few hawks are as colorful or as small as the American Kestrel.

Acrobats of the Air

Each kind of hawk has its own special flying skills. Some can soar and glide for great distances without flapping their wings. Others must flap hard to fly but are masters of fast stops and quick turns. And still others can hover over the ground like miniature helicopters. This lets them check out intended prey before diving down from the sky after it.

Opposite page:

Rough-legged Hawk.

Method of Soaring

As the hot sun warms the air near the ground the warmed air begins to rise in the shape of a bubble. While rising it draws in the surrounding cooler air, which in turn is heated and rises. The result is a balloon of warm air. As it climbs it forms a swirling doughnut of warm air called a thermal. Once a hawk is inside this thermal it can glide effortlessly and at the same time be lifted higher and higher.

Champion Sky Diver

Imagine diving through the air at 290 kilometres (180 miles) per hour. That is faster than many race cars. Believe it or not, that is how fast one kind of hawk, the Peregrine Falcon, can dive after its prey.

Hawks that do a lot of fast diving have developed a special way to protect their nostrils from the sudden rush of air as they dive. A system of plugs helps to close their nostrils off and control the amount of air that is taken into their lungs.

At one time, the Peregrine Falcon was known as the "great-footed hawk." The name is no longer used but it is easy to see where it came from.

Super Sight

Few birds can judge distances as accurately as a hawk. They do not need to because their food stays put. But a hawk's food is often on the move. And if the hawk is to catch this moving dinner, it must know where to pounce. The hawk's eyes, like those of many other animal hunters, are in the front of its head. This enables it to judge distances accurately.

Because the hawk also has very good eyesight, it can see a mouse in the grass far below as it flies over a field. With such super eyesight, the hawk has little need for a good sense of smell or for extremely keen hearing. A hawk may use these senses, but its sniffer and ears are probably not much better than yours.

These sharp eyes don't miss much. (Swainson's Hawk)

Eye Protection

The hawk depends on its eyes for survival. Without its good eyesight it could not hunt and would quickly starve. Because hawks cannot just go to the store and buy a pair of glasses if they have eye problems, they have come up with three sets of eyelids to protect their eyes.

The hawk's upper and lower eyelids look much like yours. The difference is that hawks move the lower lid up over their eye when they blink. The third eyelid moves from side to side across the eye, rather like a windshield wiper, to help clear and moisten the eye's surface.

Buteos do most of their hunting as they circle high over open fields. Even when they pause for a rest, however, they keep a sharp eye out in case an easy meal happens by. (Red-tailed Hawk)

Winged Hunters

People have favorite foods and so do hawks. Some kinds of hawks snap up grasshoppers, butterflies and other insects. Others prefer snakes, birds, rabbits or mice. And one kind of hawk, the osprey, dines mainly on fish. Whatever their choice of food, all hawks have one thing in common. They all hunt during the daytime—unlike owls, most of which hunt at night.

Hawks hunt with remarkable skill, taking mostly the unwary, sick or unskilled members of their prey. By removing the weak, they help maintain the balance of nature and ensure the survival of the healthiest animals.

Red-shouldered Hawk.

Blending In

Although hawks are skilled hunters, their prey are skilled at avoiding being caught. The hawk must therefore sneak up quickly on its prey without alarming it. For this purpose, the hawk's coloring is very useful. As a hawk flies overhead, its light underbelly helps it to blend into the sky so that it is not easily seen by animals on the ground.

Hawks that hunt by perching in trees and watching for movement can also be difficult to see. By sitting very still, they blend in with the sky from one direction while their dark back and shoulders give the appearance of a broken branch when viewed from behind.

Hawk disappearing act. A casual glance from a distance might completely miss this Sharp-shinned Hawk against the beiges and browns of the tree bark.

Hunting Tactics

If you have ever seen a hawk flying overhead, you have probably seen a hunter at work. Many hawks watch for movement on the ground as they fly. If they see a mouse or other tasty animal scurrying through the grass, they dive down and grab it with their sharp talons. The osprey uses much the same technique when hunting for fish.

Some kinds of hawks sit motionless in trees waiting for unsuspecting animals to pass by. Then—pounce!

Hawks that hunt birds use another tactic. They dive after their flying dinner and snatch it right out of the air.

Waiting for lunch. (Red-shouldered Hawk)

Talons and Toes

Like the skilled hands of a baseball player catching a ball, the hawk's feet work to grab hold of its prey. Each foot has four strong toes with sharp claws, called talons. Three toes point forward, while the fourth points back. This back toe helps in gripping—much like your thumb does when you grab something.

The hawk's strong toes serve another useful purpose as well: their firm grip allows the hawk to sleep on its perch without any danger of falling off.

The Red-tailed Hawk preys mainly on small rodents. It is the most familiar and widespread member of the buteos.

A Meat-eating Beak

All birds have beaks that help them eat their food and the hawk is no exception. Its powerful curved beak enables it to tear larger prey into chunks it can swallow.

A hawk usually eats every morsel of its prey—including fur, feathers, feet and even bones. Then its stomach goes to work sorting out food from garbage. The bits that the hawk cannot digest are formed into small round pellets and later spit up.

The osprey's hooked beak identifies it as a bird of prey.

A Ballet of Love

Hawks take only one mate each season and some even mate for life. The male and female meet during the early spring. Many hawk pairs perform a remarkable aerial ballet before mating. They dart and swoop toward each other and may even clasp each other's feet in mid-air for a few seconds. Then they swoop off and back together again. Sometimes this ballet is repeated at other times of the year by a pair of hawks who seem to be just enjoying the freedom of flying.

Master of the air. (Osprey)

Nesting

Most kinds of hawks build isolated nests high up in trees or on cliffsides. In recent years, some cliff-dwelling hawks have taken to building their homes on the tops of high-rise buildings! The city is a busy place but, high above the streets, no one will bother the hawks. And there are plenty of pigeons for a young family to eat.

Hawks that live in the prairies or in marshy areas, where trees are scarce, build their nests on the ground, hiding them carefully in the grass or in a tangle of marsh plants.

The ground-nesting Northern Harrier hides its nest well in tall marsh grasses.

There are as many kinds of nests as there are hawks. Some hawks are content to borrow nests no longer used by crows or other birds, but many build their own. Often, the male and female build it together very early in the spring. They make use of twigs, branches, dried leaves or any other materials they can find.

Some hawks make sturdy nests which they add to from year to year. On the other hand, if a safe enough place is available—a cliff perhaps or rocky hillside that few predators can get to—a hawk may not bother with a nest at all. The mother will simply lay her eggs on the bare ground.

Out of sight from above and below.
(Prairie Falcon and nestlings)

The Long, Cold Wait

The female hawk lays her eggs early in the spring. In northern areas you can sometimes see a mother hawk covered with snow as she huddles over her eggs to protect them and keep them warm.

The female has a special way of keeping her eggs warm, even in the coldest weather. As she gets ready to lay her eggs, some of her breast feathers fall out and she lines her nest with them. The bare patch left on her breast is supplied with extra blood. As she settles down on her eggs, this bare patch supplies added warmth.

Most hawks lay two to five eggs that take about a month to hatch. The female usually lays one egg every other day, but she begins sitting on them the very first day. This means that each egg hatches on a different day.

Happy hatch day. (Northern Harrier nestlings)

Thieves Beware

Although hawks are very secretive about their nests, it is usually easy to tell when one is near by the uproar most parent hawks make at the merest approach of an intruder. They screech and scream threateningly, trying to scare away the intruder—and usually succeeding. But if a determined egg or chick snatcher persists, the parents defend their nest ferociously, attacking with sharp talons and beak. A thief lucky enough to escape these protective parents will get the message: "Leave us alone or else!"

Protective parents. (Red-tailed Hawks and chick)

Out of the Eggs

For the first week of its life a baby hawk is quite helpless, barely able to lift its head. It is covered in soft down and its eyes are large and dark.

The parents feed their nestlings with tiny pieces of meat and shelter them throughout the day and night with their own bodies. At the first sign of rain the female crouches over her chicks to protect them.

In the second week in the young hawk's life, remarkable changes begin to take place. The hawk has learned to hold its head up and starts demanding food in loud, piercing squeals. Sometimes the babies become quite pushy and grab a piece of meat that is too big for them. Their watchful parent patiently helps to tear the meat into smaller pieces.

The hawks grow with amazing speed and they need plenty of food to do this. Imagine eating your own body weight in food every day. That is what some baby hawks need. Finding enough food for this hungry family keeps the hawk parents very busy!

Opposite page:

Home delivery. (Red-shouldered Hawk and chick)

Flying and Hunting Practice

By the end of their first month the young birds are ready to try flying. Usually the first flight is a short glide from their nest tree to some nearby branch. It will take some time for them to master the skills of flying and match the acrobatics of their parents. But they are eager to practice their new skill.

As the young hawks become comfortable in the air, they begin to hunt for themselves. By early summer they are ready to leave the nest and go off on their own.

Rough landing. (Red-tailed Hawk chick)

On Their Own

The first year of a young hawk's life is a difficult one. It must find enough food for itself and fight off predators who can recognize a young inexperienced bird. If it must fly south for the winter, it must also embark on a long and exhausting trip on its own.

Yet in spite of the dangers, hawks are clever birds whose will to survive is strong. If they learn their survival lessons well, they will have several families of their own and live to be as much as 10 years old.

Special Words

Down   Very soft feathers.

Habitat   The area or type of area in which an animal or plant naturally lives.

Hatch   To break out of an egg.

Mating season   The time of year during which animals come together to produce young.

Nestling   A bird that is too young to leave the nest.

Nostrils   The openings in the nose that take in air.

Predator   Animal that lives by hunting others for food.

Prey   An animal hunted by another animal for food. A bird that hunts animals for food is often called a bird of prey.

Soar   To rise higher in the air with little or no wing movement by using air currents.

Talons   Claws of a hawk or other bird of prey.

INDEX

Cover Photo: Thomas Kitchin (Valan Photos)

Photo Credits: Wilf Schurig (Valan Photos), page 4; Norman Lightfoot (Eco-Art Productions), page 7; George Peck, pages 9, 12, 28, 39; Tim Fitzharris (First Light Associated Photographers), pages 10, 20; Albert Kuhnigk (Valan Photos), pages 15, 27, 44; E. Degginger (Miller Services), page 16; Bill Ivy, page 19; National Museum of Natural Science, page 23; Vince Claerhout, page 24; Arthur Holbrook (Miller Services), page 31; J.D. Taylor (Miller Services), page 32; Mark Peck, page 35; Thomas Kitchin (Valan Photos), page 36; Barry Ranford, page 40; James Richards, page 42.